Profiles of the Presidents

GROVER
CLEVELAND

★ ★ ★

Profiles of the Presidents

GROVER CLEVELAND

by Jean Kinney Williams

Content Adviser: Sharon Farrell, Caretaker, Grover Cleveland Birthplace, Caldwell, New Jersey

Reading Adviser: Dr. Linda D. Labbo, Department of Reading Education, College of Education, The University of Georgia

COMPASS MINNESOTA

Compass Point Books
3109 West 50th Street, #115
Minneapolis, MN 55410

Visit Compass Point Books on the Internet at *www.compasspointbooks.com*
or e-mail your request to *custserv@compasspointbooks.com*

Photographs ©: White House Collection, Courtesy White House Historical Association, cover, 1;
North Wind Picture Archives, 6, 9, 16, 19, 21, 22, 23 (bottom), 29, 32, 34, 42, 43, 44, 48, 49, 54
(left), 57 (left), 58 (left), 59 (left); Hulton/Archive by Getty Images, 8, 18, 26, 38, 50, 55 (bottom), 57
(right), 58 (right); 59 (right, all); Buffalo & Erie County Historical Society, 10, 12, 13 (top); Courtesy
New York Institute of Special Education, 11; Courtesy New Jersey State Park Service, Grover Cleveland
Birth Place Historic Site, 13 (bottom); Corbis, 15, 17, 23 (top), 24, 28 (top), 31, 35, 36, 39, 40;
Bettmann/Corbis, 25, 27, 37, 41, 45; Library of Congress, 30, 55 (top); Stock Montage, 33, 47; Texas
Library & Archives Commission, 54 (top right); Bruce Burkhardt/Corbis, 54 (bottom right); Union
Pacific Historical Collection, 56 (left); Denver Public Library, Western History Collection, 56 (right).

Editors: E. Russell Primm, Emily J. Dolbear, Melissa McDaniel, and Catherine Neitge
Photo Researcher: Svetlana Zhurkina
Photo Selector: Linda S. Koutris
Designer: The Design Lab
Cartographer: XNR Productions, Inc.

Library of Congress Cataloging-in-Publication Data
Williams, Jean Kinney.
  Grover Cleveland / by Jean Kinney Williams.
      p. cm.— (Profiles of the presidents)
Summary: A biography of the twenty-second president of the United States, detailing his personal life
and public service career, from his modest beginnings as a minister's son to his two terms as president.
Includes bibliographical references and index.
Contents: A man of principles—A hard worker—Mr. mayor—From governor to president—The
bachelor president—A tough term—A private life.
  ISBN 0-7565-0269-1 (hardcover)
 1. Cleveland, Grover, 1837–1908—Juvenile literature. 2. Presidents—United States—Biography—
Juvenile literature. [1. Cleveland, Grover, 1837–1908. 2. Presidents.] I. Title. II. Series.
  E697 .W728 2003
  973.8'5'092—dc21   2002009998

Table of Contents

★ ★ ★

*NOTE: In this book, words that are defined in the glossary are
in **bold** the first time they appear in the text.*

A Man of Principles

★ ★ ★

Men, women, and ▾
children at work in a
busy textile factory in
the late 1800s

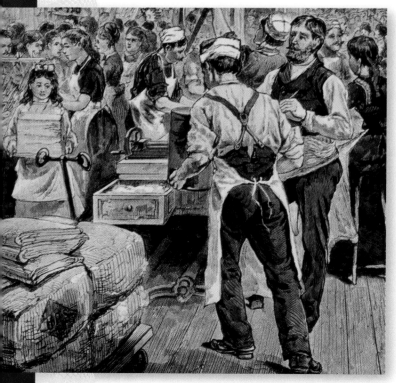

The United States was growing quickly in the 1870s. European newcomers flooded into Eastern cities. Americans from the countryside also poured into cities to work in factories or on busy docks. New industries and businesses sprouted overnight. The laws to govern these businesses often were created right along with them.

This became a problem in American politics. Business owners and political party leaders often worked together to make the laws that oversaw the businesses. They had too much influence. The party leaders often made sure that the rules favored the business owners rather than ordinary workers. Many politicians did dishonest things. A lot of Americans were disgusted by these political scandals. By the 1880s, everyday people and some politicians wanted government **reform.** In the presidential race of 1884, the Democratic Party found someone who wasn't afraid to stand up to big business and crooked politicians.

Grover Cleveland had been the mayor of Buffalo, New York, and had served as the state governor. In these jobs, Cleveland showed that he was willing to stand up for what he thought was right. Cleveland seldom sought public office during his career. Instead, others usually came to him, asking him to run. They knew about his good reputation. They thought he would be just what the people wanted. This is what happened when Grover Cleveland ran for president in 1884.

He won in a close race. During his speech after being sworn in as president, Cleveland said, "The people demand reform" in government.

So Cleveland worked for reform. He stuck to his

Grover Cleveland, the
twenty-second and
twenty-fourth
president of the
United States

principles, even when it made him unpopular. He was voted out of office in 1888. He was elected president again, however, in 1892. This made him the only president to serve two terms in office that were not one right after the other. He could have run for president again in 1896, but he was too unpopular. The Democratic Party didn't want him anymore. In time, however, people came to appreciate him. As president, Grover Cleveland once said, "What's the use of being elected or reelected unless you stand for something?"

A Hard Worker

★ ★ ★

Stephen Grover Cleveland was born on March 18, 1837, in Caldwell, New Jersey. He was the son of Richard Cleveland, a minister, and his wife, Ann Neal Cleveland. Grover was the fifth of their nine children.

▼ *The house where Grover Cleveland was born in Caldwell, New Jersey*

Rev. Richard ▲
Cleveland

The Cleveland family moved to Fayetteville, New York, near Syracuse, in 1841. Grover spent most of his childhood there. He grew up reading his father's many books, including the Bible and works by Shakespeare. He also grew up doing chores and helping take care of his younger brothers and sisters. For fun, Grover swam and fished. His father made only $1,000 a year as a minister, so the Clevelands didn't have a lot of money. The future president once said, "My training as a minister's son has been more valuable to me . . . than any other [event] in my life."

Grover Cleveland went to a public school. He had to leave school at the age of fifteen, however, to help support his family. He went to work for a Fayetteville shopkeeper. Cleveland was paid $1 per week plus meals and a room to stay in. After working in the shop for about a year, Cleveland saw no future in being a store clerk.

By then, his family had moved to another town called Holland Patent. When Cleveland learned that his father was very sick, he returned to his family. His father died less than two weeks after Grover returned home.

Grover Cleveland was again in need of a job. He was hired to be an assistant teacher at the New York Institute for the Blind. He found the place bleak and depressing and again returned home after a year.

◀ *Students making baskets at the New York Institute for the Blind*

A man who went to the same church as the Clevelands wanted to help young Grover. He offered to pay
for Grover's college education—if he would become a
minister. Cleveland, however, wanted to study law.
So instead, the man gave him a $25 loan. Cleveland
planned to travel West, to Cleveland, Ohio, for his
law studies.

On his way West, Cleveland stopped in Buffalo, New
York, to visit an uncle. Cleveland's uncle convinced him
to stay, so he would be close to his family. Cleveland lived
with his uncle and worked in the man's cattle business for

Buffalo in the 1850s ➤

a few months. Then he landed a job as a clerk in the Buffalo law office of Rodgers, Bowen and Rodgers.

At the law office, Cleveland soon proved to everyone what a hard worker he was. He studied the law and listened carefully to the other lawyers in the office. By 1859, Cleveland had become a lawyer himself. As an attorney in the Rodgers office, he made $1,000 per year. This was the same amount his father had made while supporting a wife and nine children. Grover Cleveland was now much better able to help his mother and brothers and sisters.

▲ Ann Cleveland, Grover's widowed mother

◀ Grover Cleveland, seated far left, is shown with seven of his eight brothers and sisters. One sister was not present for the photo.

Mr. Mayor

★ ★ ★

Cleveland moved to downtown Buffalo to be closer to the law office. He also became active in the Democratic Party. He tried to help elect Democrats to office. At election time, he walked the streets, urging people to vote. Cleveland proved to be loyal and well organized. Local Democratic officials rewarded him by making him an assistant **district attorney** for Erie County. A district attorney is a lawyer who argues cases in court against people accused of crimes.

By that time, America was in the middle of the Civil War (1861–1865) between the North and the South. The war had begun when some Southern states left the Union. They were afraid that newly elected president Abraham Lincoln would end slavery in the South. By 1863, the Union army needed more soldiers. They began a draft, a system that made young men become soldiers. Cleveland got a notice to serve in the army, or hire someone else to serve for him. Cleveland needed to support his mother. So he paid a Polish **immigrant** $150 to serve in the army in his place. The man survived the war.

Cleveland ran for the job of district attorney of Erie County, but he lost. Still, his reputation was growing. More and more people were learning what a talented and hard-working lawyer he was. In 1870, he ran for county sheriff. This time, he was elected.

The job of sheriff was high paying, but frustrating. A lot of tough men worked along the waterfront. They kept the county jail full. Cleveland also learned that many people who supplied the jail with food and fuel charged the

◄ *Many immigrants and African-Americans were paid to be substitute soldiers in the Union army.*

county for more supplies than they delivered. Cleveland put a stop to that, even when he had to count bags of flour himself.

Cleveland's term as sheriff ended 1873. He returned to practicing law. He also continued to impress his coworkers with his honesty and hard work. He was careful, thorough, and stubborn about right and wrong.

Cleveland often stayed up all night preparing for a case. In the morning, he would head for the courthouse with a strong cup of coffee. Though he was a hardworking lawyer, Cleveland was also fun loving and popular. He was a muscular 6 feet (183 centimeters) tall and weighed 250 pounds (113 kilograms). He enjoyed living simply, passing time in local saloons playing cards or checkers. Sometimes, he took fishing or hunting trips to the country, carrying along an old rifle he nicknamed Death and Destruction.

Cleveland (second from left) after a duck hunting trip with friends

◀ *Frances Folsom as a young woman*

In 1875, Cleveland's friend Oscar Folsom died, leaving an eleven-year-old daughter named Frances. Cleveland was always a loyal friend. He looked after the girl and helped support her.

Buffalo was a big city, and its city government was very **corrupt.** Elections were fixed. City leaders some-times took bribes from businesspeople. In 1881, Democrats wanted a **candidate** for mayor who would bring honesty and honor to Buffalo's city hall.

Grover Cleveland had been honest and honorable as a lawyer and as county sheriff. He was in the courthouse arguing a case when a group of Democrats interrupted and asked him to run for mayor. Cleveland told the judge what was going on. The judge told him, "I think you had better accept." He did.

Grover Cleveland earned a reputation for being honest and hard-working in any job or office he held.

During the campaign, Cleveland promised to cut wasteful and dishonest spending in city hall. He won the election and took office as mayor on January 1, 1882.

Just as he had pledged, Cleveland **vetoed** bills that would make bad laws for Buffalo. Cleveland insisted that the city hire companies that would do the best work for the best price. He also put a stop to city workers charging the city for their personal expenses. In 1881, more than 1,300 people in Buffalo had died after getting sick from

◄ Dirty water in the Erie Canal was causing New Yorkers to get sick in the late 1800s.

dirty water. Now, city council members wanted to pay local politicians to study the city's sewage system. Cleveland, however, refused to go along with this plan. Instead, he hired a team of experts to figure out a way to fix the sewage system. Cleveland became known as the "Veto Mayor" because he wouldn't allow spending that wasn't needed. By the end of his first year as mayor, he had saved the city $1 million.

From Governor to President

★　★　★

Grover Cleveland was just the kind of person Democrats wanted to run in the upcoming governor's race. The state government was also very corrupt. Much of this dishonesty came from **Tammany Hall,** the Democratic Party's organization in New York City.

Cleveland was not well known outside of Buffalo. Still, Democrats who wanted reform supported him for governor in 1882. Tammany Hall politicians also promised to support Cleveland. They didn't know anything about him. They believed they would be able to control him as easily as they had controlled other elected officials.

Cleveland beat the Republican candidate by more than two hundred thousand votes. On New Year's Day, 1883, exactly one year after becoming mayor of Buffalo, Cleveland was sworn in as governor of New York. That day, he told a visitor that he intended "to work for the

interests of the people of the state, regardless of party or anything else."

Governor Cleveland kept long hours reading over every bill, or proposed law, passed by the state **legislature.** Once again, he often vetoed bills. He approved bills that made the state's water healthier

▲ *This political cartoon shows corrupt Tammany Hall politicians, each pointing an accusing finger at the next man.*

Niagara Falls in ▲
the 1890s

and that established a large park at Niagara Falls.

As governor, Cleveland was also willing to take on Tammany Hall. During the campaign, many Democrats had promised government jobs to their friends if Cleveland won. After the election, those friends streamed into Cleveland's office. They were surprised to discover that the new governor only hired people who were qualified. Tammany Hall bosses came to hate Cleveland. Citizens and politicians who wanted reform loved him.

Cleveland's courage and honesty earned him respect across the nation. Once again, Democrats looking for a candidate who supported reform thought of Grover Cleveland. This time, they were looking for someone to run for president. Former Maine congressman and speaker of the house James G. Blaine was the Republican candidate. He had been involved in a bribery scandal in the 1870s. He had looked especially bad when he wrote a note about the scandal that ended, "Burn this letter!" No Democrat had been elected president since the Civil War. Yet the Democrats thought a candidate running on reform would have a good chance against Blaine.

In July 1884, Democrats met in Chicago, Illinois, and chose

▲ James G. Blaine

◄ The Democratic Convention of 1884 in Chicago

Cleveland as their candidate for president. His running mate was U.S. senator Thomas Hendricks of Indiana. An angry Tammany Hall supporter promised that Cleveland would lose the state of New York. Another Democrat, however, predicted that people from his state of Wisconsin would vote for Cleveland not just for "his integrity and judgment and iron will, but . . . most of all for the enemies he has made." Cleveland even had the support of a large

Campaign poster ➤ for running mates Grover Cleveland (left) and Thomas Hendricks

group of Republicans, nicknamed the Mugwumps, who favored reform.

Cleveland wasn't present when he became the official Democratic candidate for president. He was at his desk in Albany, New York. He heard, off in the distance, the boom of a cannon fired in celebration of his run for the presidency. Cleveland listened calmly, and then got back to work.

▲ *A political cartoon from the late 1800s using a mule to represent the Republican reformers called Mugwumps*

The *New York World* supported Cleveland for president for four reasons: "1. He is an honest man. 2. He is an honest man. 3. He is an honest man. 4. He is an honest man." Despite Cleveland's reputation, the campaign was one of the dirtiest in American history.

Democrats brought up the scandals in Blaine's past. Then Republicans pounced on information in the *Buffalo*

Evening Telegraph newspaper. The headline read, "A Terrible Tale." Grover Cleveland, the paper reported, had fathered a son out of wedlock several years earlier. Cleveland admitted that he had had an affair with the boy's mother. He wasn't sure he was the father, but he had supported the boy until he was adopted.

The campaign produced taunts such as "Blaine! Blaine! James G. Blaine! Continental liar from the state of Maine!" Another, aimed at Cleveland, was "Ma, Ma, where's my Pa? Gone to the White House, ha, ha, ha!" Cleveland made few speeches during the campaign. Instead, he tended to his duties as governor in Albany. Meanwhile, Blaine campaigned heavily across the country.

The race was too close to call as Election Day drew near. Cleveland went home to Buffalo to vote. Then he returned to Albany by train to await the results. The election was so close that it took three days of counting votes to determine that Cleveland was the winner. The real drama was in New York, which Cleveland won by just 1,149 votes. That was enough to give him New York's electoral votes, which won him the election.

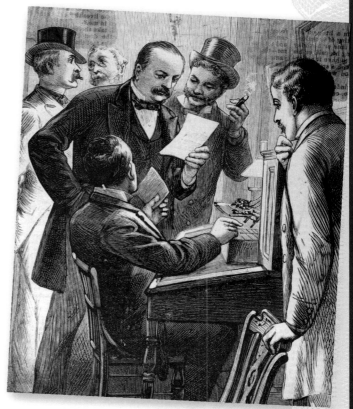

▼ *Grover Cleveland and party officials reading election results*

The inauguration of Grover Cleveland in March 1885

Amazingly, Cleveland rose from mayor of Buffalo to president of the United States in just three years. He was not excited about being elected president, though. To him, it was strictly public service: "I can see no pleasure in it and no satisfaction, only a hope that I may be of service to my people."

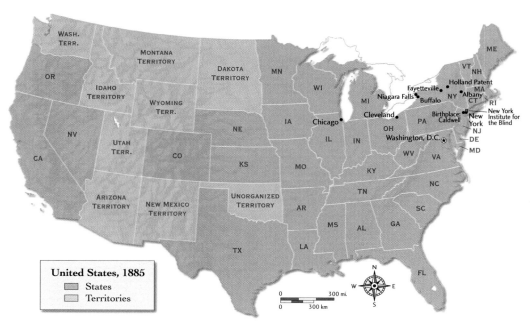

United States, 1885
- States
- Territories

A Fair Leader

★   ★   ★

Cleveland was the first Democratic president elected since 1856. One of his first challenges as president was to deal with the stream of Democrats arriving in Washington looking for government jobs. As in the past, he turned down people who weren't qualified. He also protected the jobs of good government workers who might have been replaced with politicians' friends.

▾ *President Cleveland at his desk in the White House*

Cleveland continued to work long hours. He was often at his desk by 9 A.M. and stayed until well into the night.

He read all bills passed by Congress. Cleveland was as committed as ever to vetoing bills that included wasteful spending. In his first term as president, Cleveland vetoed more than 300 bills passed by Congress. All the other presidents before him put together had vetoed only 132.

President Cleveland worked to reform the federal government. He attempted to get rid of workers who weren't needed. He tried to set better and fairer standards for hiring new workers. He also refused to grant **pensions** to hundreds of Civil War veterans who were falsely

Civil War veterans like those shown here often received pensions from the government.

claiming injuries. "Though the people support the government, the government should not support the people," he said when people protested his canceling the pensions. In 1887, Cleveland helped pass the Interstate Commerce Act. This law allowed the U.S. government to make rules for industries that cross state lines, such as railroads. Cleveland thought this would help everyday people.

He also tried to help ordinary people by forcing the railroads to give back government land they had taken. Businessmen had also stolen land that had been set aside for Native Americans. He thought Native Americans should become a part of white society. Cleveland reasoned that by giving tribes land and getting them to obey the laws of the national government, he could accomplish this.

▼ *Rose Elizabeth Cleveland*

When Cleveland first became president, his sister Rose went with him to Washington. Though she was a schoolteacher, she went to act as the White House hostess. Cleveland

The wedding of President Grover Cleveland to Frances Folsom on June 2, 1886

was served fine food each evening, but he admitted he longed for "pickled herring, Swiss cheese, and a chop." He missed the kind of food he'd eaten while relaxing in saloons in New York.

In 1885, Cleveland had a visit with Frances Folsom, his friend's daughter whom he had supported years earlier. Frances was now a college graduate and a lovely young woman. Cleveland and Frances fell in love. They were married in June 1886 when Frances was twenty-one and the president was forty-nine. It was the first wedding in the

White House. John Philip Sousa, the famous marching band director, led the U.S. Marine Corps band in the wedding march. Thousands of citizens crowded the White House lawn hoping to glimpse the couple.

Mrs. Cleveland became the youngest first lady ever, and her marriage to the president was a national event. Grover Cleveland was a loving husband. The new couple enjoyed spending time at Oak View, their private home in the nearby neighborhood of Georgetown. Another happy event for Americans in 1886 was the unveiling of the 150-foot (46-meter) Statue of Liberty in New York Harbor.

◀ *The Clevelands at Oak View*

Merchant ships ▲ unloaded imported goods along South Street in New York.

As the presidential campaign of 1888 drew near, the biggest issue was the **tariff.** A tariff is a tax on items that are brought into or shipped out of a country for sale. American businesses wanted a high tariff because it made foreign goods cost more. That made people buy more American goods. Poorer people, such as factory workers and farmers, wanted a low tariff so the things they needed wouldn't cost so much.

Cleveland thought the high tariff was unfair because it helped business owners, while forcing workers with low wages to pay more for products. "The [gap] between employers and the employed is constantly widening," Cleveland told Congress in 1887. In 1888, Congress lowered the tariff, but only slightly.

In the presidential election of 1888, Cleveland was running against Benjamin Harrison of Indiana. Harrison was a former U.S. sena-tor and the grandson of the ninth president, William Henry Harrison. Republicans fought hard for Harrison, who spoke from his front porch in Indianapolis. Cleveland continued with his duties as president. He made little attempt to campaign. If he had explained his views on the tariff, the outcome of the election might have been different.

▼ *This 1888 Democratic campaign poster for Cleveland and his running mate, Allen Thurman, focused on their plan to lower high import tariffs.*

Benjamin Harrison, the ▶
twenty-third president
of the United States

On Election Day, Cleveland actually won the popular vote by about 100,000 out of 11 million votes. Harrison, however, had more electoral votes—233 to 168. According to the U.S. Constitution, that made Harrison the next president.

Cleveland was glad to leave the presidency. His wife felt differently. She told a White House servant to take good care of the household because, "I want to find everything just as it is now when we come back again."

First Lady Frances Cleveland was confident that she and her husband would be returning to the White House.

A Tough Term

★ ★ ★

The Baby Ruth candy bar was named for the Clevelands' baby daughter, Ruth.

After leaving office, Cleveland moved to New York City, where he worked for a law firm. On October 3, 1891, Grover and Frances Cleveland welcomed their first daughter, Ruth, into the world.

Cleveland bought a summer home called Gray Gables in Massachusetts. The family spent long vacations there, and Cleveland fished to his heart's content.

Though his life was more relaxing, Cleveland kept an eye on politics. He was dismayed as Congress raised tariffs higher than they had ever been. Congress also increased the pensions of Civil War veterans. When Cleveland left office, the government was taking in more money than it was spending. It didn't take long for President Harrison and Congress to spend that extra money.

Cleveland decided to run for president against Harrison in 1892. Democrats jumped at the chance to have him as their candidate. They chose Adlai E. Stevenson, a former congressman from Illinois, as his running mate. A third candidate was also in the presidential race. A lawyer from

▼ *Running mates Grover Cleveland and Adlai E. Stevenson in 1892*

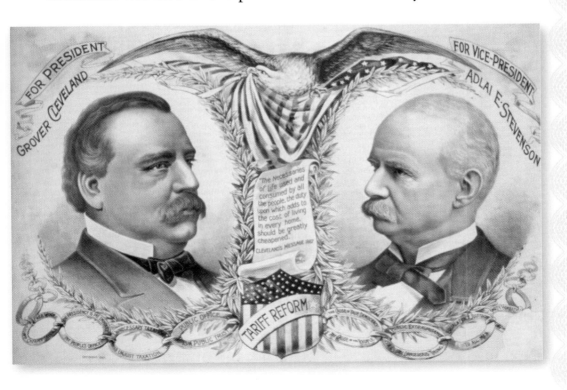

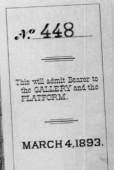

N.° 448

This will admit Bearer to the SENATE wing of the Capitol.

MARCH 4, 1893.

INAUGURATION OF THE President of the United States.

MARCH 4, 1893.

CARD OF ADMISSION

NO. 448

Levi P. Morton
Vice President and
President of
United States Senate.

Wm Eaton
M. W. Ransom
Fred Lee Th.....
Committee of Arrangements.

N.° 448

This will admit Bearer to the GALLERY and the PLATFORM.

MARCH 4, 1893.

A ticket to the second inauguration of Grover Cleveland

Iowa, James Weaver, was running as a member of the Populist Party.

The presidential race was fairly quiet. When Benjamin Harrison's wife died in October 1892, he stopped campaigning entirely. To show respect, Cleveland did the same. Cleveland won the election easily. He received nearly five hundred thousand more votes than Harrison. Weaver came in a distant third.

Cleveland was sworn in as the twenty-fourth president on March 4, 1893. He was ready to serve again.

Cleveland's second term was much more challenging than his first. Just as he was entering office, the economy took a turn for the worse. The country went into a severe economic **depression.** Businesses failed, and many people lost their jobs.

Cleveland believed that the Sherman Silver Purchase Act of 1890 was hurting the economy. This law required the U.S. government to buy millions of ounces of silver each month. Cleveland asked Congress to overturn the act. They did, but the issue split the Democratic Party. Many southern and western Democrats, who benefited from silver mining in their areas, turned against Cleveland.

◄ This cartoon, mocking Cleveland's financial policy, shows Secretary of the Treasury John G. Carlisle riding a bicycle with one gold coin and one silver coin in the place of wheels.

The depression continued to worsen. Cleveland didn't think that the government should give needy people money directly. He thought that the best way to help people was to get them back to work. The only way to do that was to improve the economy. Cleveland's repeal of the Silver Act didn't improve the economy. Instead, bands of ragged men without jobs wandered the country.

Many workers became upset with Cleveland because of how he handled a major **strike.** In a strike, people refuse to work until their wages or working conditions improve. In the summer of 1894, strikes among low-paid workers were breaking out everywhere. One of the worst was in Chicago, where George Pullman, the wealthy owner of a company that made railroad sleeping cars for trains, lowered wages for his workers. The Pullman workers went on strike.

Other railroad workers led by a union leader named Eugene V. Debs joined the Pullman strike. Striking railroad workers

Eugene V. Debs, president of the American Railway Union

blocked railroad tracks, preventing trains from moving.
They shut down the railroad system all across the country.
The police tried to control strikers who threw rocks or
bricks and set railroad cars on fire.

The burning of six hundred freight cars during the Pullman strike of 1894

U.S. attorney general Richard Olney was on the
side of the railroad owners. He explained to President
Cleveland that the strikers were preventing U.S. mail
delivery, especially in Chicago. That got Cleveland's

National Guardsmen firing at strikers in Chicago on July 7, 1894

attention: "If it takes the entire army and navy of the United States to deliver a postal card in Chicago, that card will be delivered," he declared.

In July, federal troops arrived in Chicago. By the time the violence ended, twelve people were dead and hundreds had been injured. Railroad workers returned to work, and Debs was arrested. Cleveland, however, was no longer a hero to working people.

There were foreign policy successes during Cleveland's term. Some U.S. businessmen had grown wealthy in Hawaii, which was then an independent kingdom. In 1893, a businessman named Sanford Dole led a revolt that knocked Queen Liliuokalani out of power.

◄ *Liliuokalani, queen of Hawaii*

Dole asked that the U.S. government take over Hawaii. Cleveland thought this would be unfair to native Hawaiians, and he refused.

Cleveland also showed that he could be tough when he handled a problem in South America. In 1895, British Guiana (present-day Guyana), which was controlled by Great Britain, was not respecting its border with Venezuela. Cleveland threatened Great Britain with war unless it agreed to let an outside panel decide what the border actually was. Great Britain agreed to Cleveland's demands.

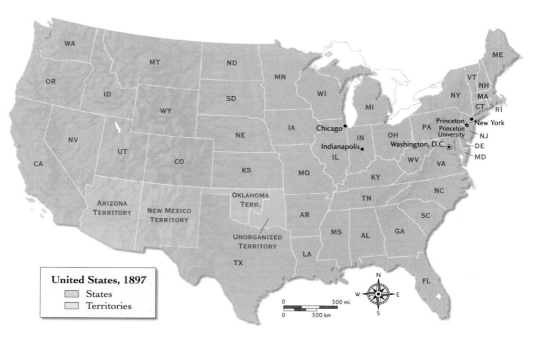

United States, 1897
☐ States
☐ Territories

Cleveland also had some happy moments in the White House, such as when Frances Cleveland gave birth to two more daughters. In 1893, Esther Cleveland became the first baby born in the White House. Her sister Marion followed two years later.

By the end of Cleveland's term in 1896, the U.S. economy was still weak. His actions during the Pullman strike had made him unpopular with certain workers. Overturning the Silver Purchase Act had made him unpopular with some of his fellow Democrats. When Democrats gathered to choose a presidential candidate that year, South Carolina's senator Ben Tillman called Cleveland's presidency "undemocratic and tyrannical."

The Democrats withdrew their support from Cleveland. Instead they chose William Jennings Bryan, a Nebraska

▼ *William Jennings Bryan giving a speech*

President William ▲ McKinley congressman with a colorful speaking style. Bryan fought hard for the presidency but lost to the Republican candidate, William McKinley.

A Private Life

★ ★ ★

Cleveland felt a mixture of relief and disgrace at the end of his presidency. As soon as his term ended, he moved to Princeton, New Jersey. Cleveland became involved with Princeton University, giving lectures and helping oversee the school. He wrote and sometimes did legal work. He gave up public life almost entirely.

▼ Grover Cleveland (right) at a function at Princeton University

Though nearly sixty years old, Cleveland enjoyed his young family. His first son, Richard, was born in 1897. A second son, Francis, followed in 1903.

Cleveland was grief

stricken when his daughter Ruth came down with a deadly disease called diphtheria and died in 1904. She was twelve years old.

By 1908, the health of the energetic former president was failing. Once hearty and robust, he was becoming frail and thin. He died at home on June 24, at the age of seventy-one. His last words were, "I have tried so hard to do right."

When Cleveland left the White House in 1897, many Americans hated him. Over time, however, people had remembered that he was a good public servant. When he died, people all across the nation mourned him. He was, historians now agree, a strong and effective leader when the United States needed one.

Grover and Frances Cleveland with their four children in 1907. Their oldest daughter, Ruth, died three years before this picture was taken.

GLOSSARY

★ ★ ★

candidate—someone running for office in an election

corrupt—dishonest

depression—a time when businesses do badly and many people become poor

district attorney—a lawyer who is in charge of the cases against people accused of crimes

immigrant—a person who moves from one country to live permanently in another

legislature—the part of government that makes or changes laws

pensions—money paid regularly to people who have retired from work

reform—an improvement, or the correcting of something that is unsatisfactory

strike—when workers refuse to work, hoping to force their company to agree to their demands

Tammany Hall—the center of the Democratic Party in New York City in the 1800s; it was famous for being corrupt

tariff—tax placed on certain foreign goods entering a country

vetoed—refused to approve, which prevented a measure from taking effect

GROVER CLEVELAND'S LIFE AT A GLANCE

★ ★ ★

PERSONAL

Nickname:	None
Birth date:	March 18, 1837
Birthplace:	Caldwell, New Jersey
Father's name:	Richard Falley Cleveland
Mother's name:	Ann Neal Cleveland
Education:	No formal education
Wife's name:	Frances Folsom Cleveland (1864–1947)
Married:	June 2, 1886
Children:	Ruth Cleveland (1891–1904); Esther Cleveland (1893–1980); Marion Cleveland (1895–1977); Richard Folsom Cleveland (1897–1974); Francis Grover Cleveland (1903–1995)
Died:	June 24, 1908, in Princeton, New Jersey
Buried:	Princeton, New Jersey

PUBLIC

Occupation before presidency:	Teacher, lawyer
Occupation after presidency:	Lecturer
Military service:	None
Other government positions:	Assistant district attorney of Erie County; sheriff of Erie County; mayor of Buffalo; governor of New York
Political party:	Democrat
Vice presidents:	Thomas A. Hendricks (1885–1889); Adlai E. Stevenson (1893–1897)
Dates in office:	March 4, 1885–March 4, 1889; and March 4, 1893–March 4, 1897
Presidential opponents:	James G. Blaine (Republican), 1884; Benjamin Harrison (Republican), 1888 and 1892
Number of votes (Electoral College):	4,879,507 of 9,729,800 (219 of 401), 1884; 5,537,857 of 10,984,986 (168 of 401), 1888; 5,555,426 of 11,768,362 (277 of 422), 1892
Writings:	*Presidential Problems* (1904)

★

Grover Cleveland's Cabinet

Secretary of state:
  Thomas F. Bayard (1885–1889)
  Walter Q. Gresham (1893–1895)
  Richard Olney (1895–1897)

Secretary of the treasury:
  Daniel Manning (1885–1887)
  Charles S. Fairchild (1887–1889)
  John G. Carlisle (1893–1897)

Secretary of war:
  William C. Endicott (1885–1889)
  Daniel S. Lamont (1893–1897)

Attorney general:
  Augustus H. Garland (1885–1889)
  Richard Olney (1893–1895)
  Judson Harmon (1895–1897)

Postmaster general:
  William F. Vilas (1885–1888)
  Donald M. Dickinson (1888–1889)
  Wilson S. Bissell (1893–1895)
  William L. Wilson (1895–1897)

Secretary of the navy:
  William C. Whitney (1885–1889)
  Hilary A. Herbert (1893–1897)

Secretary of the interior:
  Lucius Q. C. Lamar (1885–1888)
  William F. Vilas (1888–1889)
  Hoke Smith (1893–1896)
  David R. Francis (1896–1897)

Secretary of agriculture:
  Norman J. Colman (1889)
  Julius Sterling Morton (1893–1897)

GROVER CLEVELAND'S LIFE AND TIMES

★ ★ ★

CLEVELAND'S LIFE	WORLD EVENTS

		1836	Texans defeat Mexican troops at San Jacinto after a deadly battle at the Alamo (above)
March 18, Stephen Grover Cleveland is born in Caldwell, New Jersey (below)	1837	1837	American banker J. P. Morgan is born
	1840	1840	Auguste Rodin, famous sculptor of *The Thinker* (below), is born

CLEVELAND'S LIFE

WORLD EVENTS

1850

1860

1848   *The Communist Manifesto,* by German writer Karl Marx, is widely distributed

1852   American Harriet Beecher Stowe (below) publishes *Uncle Tom's Cabin*

Becomes a teacher at the New York Institute for the Blind   1853

1858   English scientist Charles Darwin (right) presents his theory of evolution

Becomes a lawyer   1859

1860   Austrian composer Gustav Mahler is born in Kalischt (now in Austria)

Pays a Polish immigrant to take his place in the army during the Civil War   1863

CLEVELAND'S LIFE

Elected sheriff of Erie   1870
County

1870

WORLD EVENTS

1865   *Tristan and Isolde,* by German composer Richard Wagner, opens in Munich

Lewis Carroll writes *Alice's Adventures in Wonderland*

1868   Louisa May Alcott publishes *Little Women*

1869   The transcontinental railroad across the United States is completed (left)

1870   John D. Rockefeller founds the Standard Oil Company

1876   The Battle of the Little Bighorn is a victory for Native Americans defending their homes in the West against General George Custer (above)

Alexander Graham Bell uses the first telephone to speak to his assistant, Thomas Watson

1877   German inventor Nikolaus A. Otto works on what will become the internal combustion engine for automobiles

CLEVELAND'S LIFE

WORLD EVENTS

1879   Electric lights are invented

1880

Elected mayor of   1882
Buffalo, New York

1882   Thomas Edison builds a power station

Sworn in as governor   1883
of New York

Presidential Election Results:		*Popular Votes*	*Electoral Votes*
1884	*Grover Cleveland*	*4,879,507*	*219*
	James G. Blaine	*4,850,293*	*182*

1884   Mark Twain publishes *The Adventures of Hucklelberry Finn*

Cleveland's marriage   1886
to Frances Folsom
is the first wedding
in the White House
(above)

1886   Bombing in Haymarket Square, Chicago, due to labor unrest (below)

Dedicates the Statue of
Liberty in New York

Wins more popular   1888
votes than Benjamin
Harrison in the
presidential election
but loses because
Harrison beats him in
the electoral college

CLEVELAND'S LIFE

1890

Presidential Election Results:		Popular Votes	Electoral Votes
1892	Grover Cleveland	5,555,426	277
	Benjamin Harrison	5,182,690	145
	James B. Weaver	1,029,846	22

1893 March 4, Cleveland is sworn in as president, becoming the only president to serve two terms that do not follow one after the other

May, an economic depression hits the country

1894 The Pullman strike stops the country's railroad system; Cleveland sends in federal troops to end the strike (below)

WORLD EVENTS

1891 The Roman Catholic Church publishes the encyclical *Rerum Novarum,* which supports the rights of labor

1893 Women gain voting privileges in New Zealand, the first country to take such a step

1896 The Olympic Games (above) are held for the first time in recent history, in Athens, Greece

CLEVELAND'S LIFE

Moves to Princeton, 1897–
New Jersey; becomes 1908
involved with Princeton
University, giving lectures
and helping oversee
school affairs

Cleveland's daughter, 1904
Ruth, dies of diphtheria
at age twelve

June 24, dies in Princeton, 1908
New Jersey

WORLD EVENTS

1899   Isadora Duncan (above),
one of the founders of
modern dance, makes her
debut in Chicago

1903   Brothers Orville and
Wilbur Wright success-
fully fly a powered
airplane (above)

1909   The National Association
for the Advancement of
Colored People (NAACP)
is founded

1900

UNDERSTANDING GROVER CLEVELAND AND HIS PRESIDENCY

★ ★ ★

IN THE LIBRARY

Gaines, Ann Graham. *Grover Cleveland: Our Twenty-Second and Twenty-Fourth President.* Chanhassen, Minn.: The Child's World, 2002.

Joseph, Paul. *Grover Cleveland.* Minneapolis: Checkerboard Library, 2001.

ON THE WEB

The White House—Grover Cleveland
http://www.whitehouse.gov/history/presidents/gc2224.html
To find out more about Cleveland's life and presidency

First Inaugural Address
http://www.bartleby.com/124/pres37.html
To read the speech Cleveland gave after being sworn in on March 4, 1885

Grover Cleveland Home Page
http://www.rain.org/~turnpike/grover/Main.html
To learn more about the life of Grover Cleveland

Political Cartoons
http://www.history.ohio-state.edu/projects/uscartoons/Cleveland1900.htm
To see some cartoons about
Cleveland and the politics of his times

CLEVLAND HISTORIC SITES
ACROSS THE COUNTRY

Birthplace of Grover Cleveland
207 Bloomfield Avenue
Caldwell, NJ 07006
973/226-0001
To see where Cleveland was born

Grover Cleveland Grave Site
Princeton Cemetery
29 Greenview Avenue
Princeton, NJ 08542-3316
609/924-1369
To visit Cleveland's burial place

THE U.S. PRESIDENTS
(Years in Office)

★ ★ ★

1. **George Washington**
   (March 4, 1789–March 3, 1797)
2. **John Adams**
   (March 4, 1797–March 3, 1801)
3. **Thomas Jefferson**
   (March 4, 1801–March 3, 1809)
4. **James Madison**
   (March 4, 1809–March 3, 1817)
5. **James Monroe**
   (March 4, 1817–March 3, 1825)
6. **John Quincy Adams**
   (March 4, 1825–March 3, 1829)
7. **Andrew Jackson**
   (March 4, 1829–March 3, 1837)
8. **Martin Van Buren**
   (March 4, 1837–March 3, 1841)
9. **William Henry Harrison**
   (March 6, 1841–April 4, 1841)
10. **John Tyler**
    (April 6, 1841–March 3, 1845)
11. **James K. Polk**
    (March 4, 1845–March 3, 1849)
12. **Zachary Taylor**
    (March 5, 1849–July 9, 1850)
13. **Millard Fillmore**
    (July 10, 1850–March 3, 1853)
14. **Franklin Pierce**
    (March 4, 1853–March 3, 1857)
15. **James Buchanan**
    (March 4, 1857–March 3, 1861)
16. **Abraham Lincoln**
    (March 4, 1861–April 15, 1865)
17. **Andrew Johnson**
    (April 15, 1865–March 3, 1869)

18. **Ulysses S. Grant**
    (March 4, 1869–March 3, 1877)
19. **Rutherford B. Hayes**
    (March 4, 1877–March 3, 1881)
20. **James Garfield**
    (March 4, 1881–Sept 19, 1881)
21. **Chester Arthur**
    (Sept 20, 1881–March 3, 1885)
22. Grover Cleveland
    (March 4, 1885–March 3, 1889)
23. **Benjamin Harrison**
    (March 4, 1889–March 3, 1893)
24. Grover Cleveland
    (March 4, 1893–March 3, 1897)
25. **William McKinley**
    (March 4, 1897–
    September 14, 1901)
26. **Theodore Roosevelt**
    (September 14, 1901–
    March 3, 1909)
27. **William Howard Taft**
    (March 4, 1909–March 3, 1913)
28. **Woodrow Wilson**
    (March 4, 1913–March 3, 1921)
29. **Warren G. Harding**
    (March 4, 1921–August 2, 1923)
30. **Calvin Coolidge**
    (August 3, 1923–March 3, 1929)
31. **Herbert Hoover**
    (March 4, 1929–March 3, 1933)
32. **Franklin D. Roosevelt**
    (March 4, 1933–April 12, 1945)

33. **Harry S. Truman**
    (April 12, 1945–
    January 20, 1953)
34. **Dwight D. Eisenhower**
    (January 20, 1953–
    January 20, 1961)
35. **John F. Kennedy**
    (January 20, 1961–
    November 22, 1963)
36. **Lyndon B. Johnson**
    (November 22, 1963–
    January 20, 1969)
37. **Richard M. Nixon**
    (January 20, 1969–
    August 9, 1974)
38. **Gerald R. Ford**
    (August 9, 1974–
    January 20, 1977)
39. **James Earl Carter**
    (January 20, 1977–
    January 20, 1981)
40. **Ronald Reagan**
    (January 20, 1981–
    January 20, 1989)
41. **George H. W. Bush**
    (January 20, 1989–
    January 20, 1993)
42. **William Jefferson Clinton**
    (January 20, 1993–
    January 20, 2001)
43. **George W. Bush**
    (January 20, 2001–)

INDEX

★ ★ ★

Index

ABOUT THE AUTHOR

Jean Kinney Williams lives and writes in Cincinnati, Ohio. Her nonfiction books for children include *Matthew Henson: Polar Adventurer* and a series of books about American religions. She is also the author of *The Pony Express, African-Americans in the Colonies, Ulysses S. Grant,* and *Cook: James Cook Charts the Pacific Ocean.*

Fiber

George Ivanoff

Smart Apple Media
P.O. Box 3263
Mankato, MN, 56002

First published in 2011 by
MACMILLAN EDUCATION AUSTRALIA PTY LTD
15–19 Claremont St, South Yarra, Australia 3141

Visit our web site at www.macmillan.com.au or go directly to www.macmillanlibrary.com.au

Associated companies and representatives throughout the world.

Copyright Text © George Ivanoff 2011

Library of Congress Cataloging-in-Publication Data has been applied for.

Publisher: Carmel Heron
Commissioning Editor: Niki Horin
Managing Editor: Vanessa Lanaway
Editor: Emma Short
Proofreader: Georgina Garner
Designer: Kerri Wilson
Page layout: Cath Pirret Design
Photo researcher: Sarah Johnson (management: Debbie Gallagher)
Illustrator: Leigh Hedstrom, Flee Illustration
Production Controller: Vanessa Johnson

Manufactured in China by Macmillan Production (Asia) Ltd.
Kwun Tong, Kowloon, Hong Kong
Supplier Code: CP December 2010

Acknowledgments
The author and the publisher are grateful to the following for permission to reproduce copyright material:

Front cover photograph: Boy eating vegetables, Dreamstime/Matka_wariatka

Photographs courtesy of: Dreamstime, 15 (water), 28 (legumes), /Creativefire, 24, /Carolborreda, 26, /Cybernesco, 7 (middle), /
Dragon_fang, 29, /Dana, 16, /Digitoll, 9 (white rice), /Draconus, 9 (almonds), /Icefront, 7 (bottom left), /Jimh12345, 9 (white bread),
/Ksena2009, 9 (rye bread), /Monkey Business Images, 5, 21, 25, /Moth, 12, /Nmonckton, 28 (fruit, nuts), /Onlyfabrizio, 15 (kidney
beans, cannellini beans), /Petro, 30, /Picstudio, 15 (peas), /Scyza, 28 (bread), /Alexander Silaev, 3, 7 (top), /Sqback, 9 (banana),
/Ukrphoto, 6 (bottom), /Valentyn75, 7 (bottom right), /West1, 11; Getty Images/Cole Group, 22; iStockphoto/Jesper Elgaard,
19, /Lauri Patterson, 28 (vegetables); Photolibrary/Banana Stock, 27, /FoodCollection, 9 (barley), /Imagesource, 17; Pixmac/
a4stockphotos, 6 (top), Science Photo Library/Eye of Science, 10; Shutterstock/kRie, 14, /Monkey Business Images, 4, 8, /Morgan
Lane Photography, 6 (middle), /szefei, 9 (biscuit).

Contents

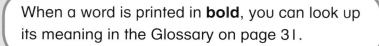

When a word is printed in **bold**, you can look up its meaning in the Glossary on page 31.

What's in My Food?

Your food is made up of **nutrients**. Nutrients help your body work, grow, and stay alive.

Nutrients give you **energy** so you can be active.

Different types of food contain different types of nutrients. A **balanced diet** includes foods with the right amount of nutrients for your body.

A balanced diet helps keep your body healthy.

What Nutrients Are in My Food?

There are many different types of nutrients in your food. They include proteins, carbohydrates, fats, fiber, minerals, and vitamins.

Protein in meat, poultry, eggs, and fish helps your body grow and heal.

Carbohydrates in bread and pasta give your body energy.

Fats in fish and olive oil give your body energy and help it stay healthy.

Fiber in bread and vegetables
helps your body **digest** food.

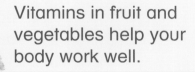

Vitamins in fruit and
vegetables help your
body work well.

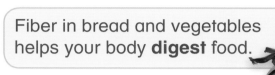

Minerals in milk and
meat help your body
grow and stay healthy.

Fiber

Fiber is a nutrient that is found in many foods. It keeps your body healthy. Adults need to eat more fiber than children to stay healthy.

To determine how much fiber children need each day, take their age and divide it by 10.

Age: 7
This person needs to eat about 0.7 ounces (17 g) of fiber every day.

Different types of food have different amounts of fiber.
These foods each contain 0.6 ounces (16 g) of fiber —

1 whole-grain
wheat cracker

$\frac{1}{4}$ cup of
cooked barley

2 slices of white bread

$\frac{1}{2}$ banana

$\frac{2}{3}$ slice of rye bread

$1\frac{1}{2}$ cups of cooked
white rice

12 almonds

What is Fiber?

Fiber is sometimes called roughage (*ruff-ij*). It is found in plants. Fiber is so small that you need a microscope to see it.

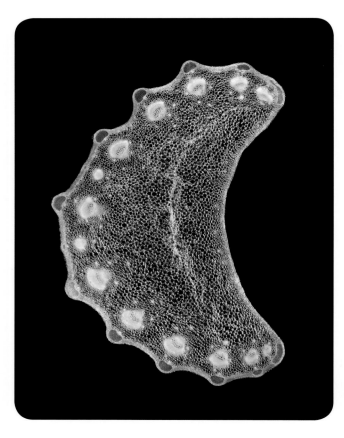

This photo shows the **cells** inside a celery stalk, which contain fiber.

The more that foods are **processed**, the less fiber they contain. Wheat grains are used to make white bread, but most of the fiber is removed.

Whole-grain bread is healthier than white bread because it is less processed and has more fiber.

Fiber is really a type of carbohydrate. It is different from other carbohydrates, such as sugar. Your body cannot digest fiber like other carbohydrates.

Nutritional Information

Servings per package: 1.5
Serving Size: 100g

	Per 100g
Energy	59kcal*
Protein	3g
Total Fat	0g
*Saturated fat	0g
Cholesterol	0mg
Carbohydrate	8.5g
Dietary Fiber	2.1g
Calcium	5.8mg
Sodium	5mg
Magnesium	1.9mg
Potassium	208.6mg
Vitamin B2	0.2mg
Vitamin B3	1.0mg
Zinc	0.6mg

*1kcal = 4.2kJ

Fiber is listed separately from carbohydrates on the list of nutrients contained in food products.

There are two types of fiber: soluble fiber and insoluble fiber. Both types of fiber pass through your body and come out with the **waste**.

Fiber does not break down in your stomach like other nutrients from food.

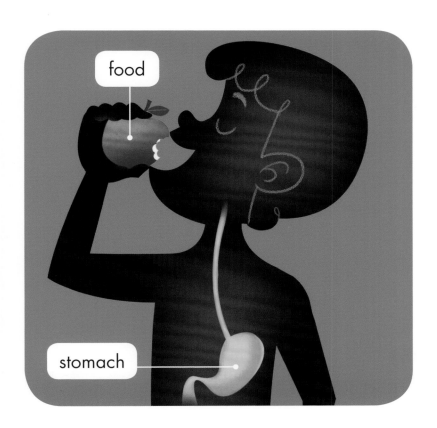

Soluble Fiber

Soluble fiber **dissolves** in water and attaches to waste in your body. It makes the waste softer and helps it pass through your body more quickly. Soluble fiber can be found in many fruits, grains, and legumes.

You need to drink plenty of water to dissolve the fiber in your body.

Insoluble Fiber

Insoluble fiber does not dissolve in water. It attaches to waste in your body, making it larger. This also helps the waste pass through your body.

Peas, kidney beans, and white beans contain insoluble fiber.

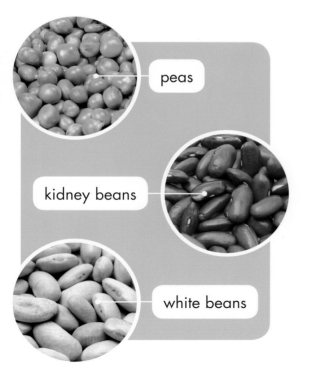

peas

kidney beans

white beans

You need to drink plenty of water to help insoluble fiber pass through your body.

What Does Fiber Do?

Fiber helps your **digestive system** work well. It helps your body get rid of waste more easily.

Fiber helps you digest food well, which helps you feel happy and healthy.

Fiber changes the way that your body **absorbs** some nutrients. This affects the **blood sugar** and **cholesterol** in your body.

Eating enough fiber will help you stay at a healthy weight.

Fiber Keeps Me Healthy

Fiber makes the waste from your digestive system softer and larger. This makes it quicker and easier for waste to pass through your body.

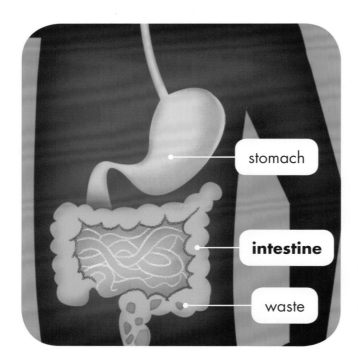

stomach

intestine

waste

If waste takes too long to pass out of your body, **constipation** can occur.

Fiber Helps Control My Blood Sugar

Fiber helps your body absorb sugar more slowly.
This controls the amount of blood sugar in your body.

If you have too much or too little blood sugar, your
energy level changes, too. Low blood sugar makes
it hard to concentrate.

Fiber Lowers My Cholesterol

Fiber helps lower cholesterol in your blood. It traps some of the cholesterol in the food your stomach digests. This cholesterol passes out of your body with the waste.

Too much cholesterol in your blood can cause heart **disease**.

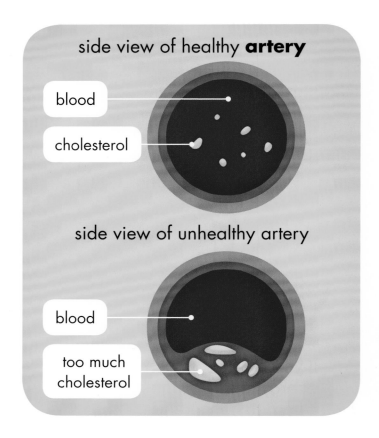

side view of healthy **artery**

blood

cholesterol

side view of unhealthy artery

blood

too much cholesterol

Fiber Helps Me Control My Weight

Foods with fiber are more filling than foods without fiber. So if you eat a lot of fiber, you are less likely to overeat. Soluble fiber also makes you feel full for longer.

Eating enough fiber can help you keep a healthy weight and stay active.

Which Foods Contain Fiber?

Fiber is found only in foods made from plants. There is no fiber in meat, poultry, fish, eggs, or dairy foods.

All of these foods are made from plants and contain fiber.

Foods with fiber are part of a balanced diet. Other foods also have nutrients that your body needs, such as vitamins and minerals. You need to eat these foods, too.

A balanced diet includes many different kinds of foods, as well as water.

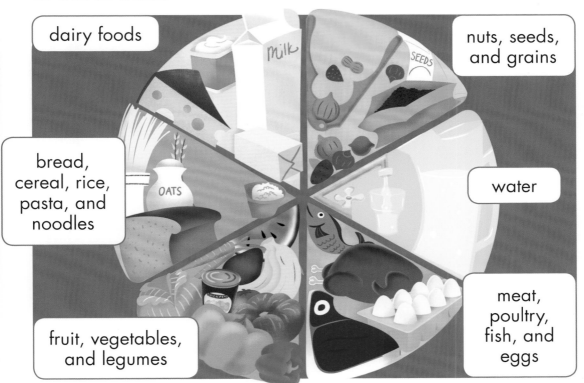

dairy foods

nuts, seeds, and grains

bread, cereal, rice, pasta, and noodles

water

fruit, vegetables, and legumes

meat, poultry, fish, and eggs

Fiber Is in Fruit and Vegetables

Fruit and vegetables contain fiber, especially in their skins. Dried fruit has as much fiber as fresh fruit.

Pears contain a lot of fiber, especially if you eat the skin, too.

Fruit and vegetable juices have less fiber than whole fruit and vegetables. This is because the skin is removed to make the juice.

It is healthier to eat whole fruit and vegetables than to drink fruit and vegetable juices.

Fiber Is in Soy Products

Soybeans contain fiber. Soy products, such as soy milk and tofu, are made from soybeans. They also contain fiber.

soy sauce

soy milk

tofu

soybeans

All these soy products contain fiber.

Fiber Is in Nuts, Seeds, and Grains

Nuts and seeds contain fiber. Grains, such as wheat, rice, and oats, also contain fiber. These grains are used to make bread, pasta, and breakfast cereals.

Peanut butter contains fiber, as well as protein and carbohydrates.

How Can I Get More Fiber in My Diet?

Here are some ways to get more fiber in your diet.

Eat whole-grain bread instead of white bread.

Add legumes such as chickpeas or lentils to your meals

Don't peel vegetables—eat their skins too.

Snack on nuts and dried fruit instead of candy.

If you need more fiber in your diet, increase it slowly, over time. You need to drink a lot of water, too.

If you increase the amount of fiber you eat too quickly, it might make you feel sick.

What Happens if I Don't Eat Fiber?

If you don't eat fiber, your body can't get rid of waste easily. Your blood sugar level will go up and down too quickly. Your blood will absorb too much cholesterol.

Not eating enough fiber can cause many health problems, such as low energy levels.

low energy

Glossary

absorbs	takes in
artery	vessel that carries blood around your body
balanced diet	a healthy selection of food that you eat
blood sugar	sugar in your blood
cells	the smallest living parts of a living thing
cholesterol	a substance in your blood and brain
constipation	build up of waste in your intestine
digest	to break down food in your body
digestive system	the parts of your body that digest food, absorb nutrients, and get rid of waste
disease	an illness or sickness
dissolves	combines with a liquid such as water
energy	the ability to be active
intestine	the part of your body that carries waste
nutrients	the healthy parts of food that you need to live
processed	changed in some way
waste	unused material in your digestive system that passes out of your body

Index